Drenched Uniforms and Battered Badges

How Dayton Police Emerged from the 1913 Flood

Stephen C. Grismer

Published by
Dayton Police History Foundation, Inc.

This book was produced with
the generous assistance of
Curt Dalton, editor
Dayton History Books Online

The contents of this book are the author's own research
and interpretation of this aspect of history.

Contributing editors, Lou Grieco & Michael Sammons

Cover photograph and images
on pages 17, 23, 31, 85 & 101
by Amy M. Simpson
Copyright © July 2013 by
Dayton Police History Foundation, Inc.

Library of Congress Control Number: 2013942457

ISBN-10: 0989530205
ISBN-13: 978-0-9895302-0-0

Produced in the United States of America

10 9 8 7 6 5 4 3 2

Published by
DPH Foundation, Inc.
P.O. Box 293157
Dayton OH 45429-9157
www.DaytonPoliceHistory.org

Dedication

This book is dedicated to my wife, **Terrie.**
She possesses limitless patience, genuine understanding
and a giving nature unlike anyone else in my life.

In Memory of

Scott Stimmel
Dayton Mounted Patrol Sergeant
&
Bob Keen
Dayton Fraternal Order of Police
Historian & Archivist

Acknowledgments

In addition to my better half, Terrie, who willingly reviewed my countless story revisions, many others deserve recognition for their contributions to *Drenched Uniforms and Battered Badges*.

This account of the 1913 Flood was initiated simply to satisfy my interest – a curiosity that soon developed into a story and one of greater length than anticipated – but it would never have been produced as a book had it not been for the encouragement, mentoring and hands-on assistance of **Curt Dalton**. He provided additional research and freely gave his personal time.

Veteran journalist, **Lou Grieco**, a Dayton Daily News staff writer, graciously edited my account of the events under deadline. He is a true friend. Dayton Officer **Amy Simpson**, when not on police patrol, is a talented artist and photographer. She has an eye for lighting and uncommon angles. Two other police officers took the time to pose for her, wearing period police uniforms: Dayton Officer **Derric McDonald** (Part 1; page 17) and Riverside Officer **Kyle Treon** (Part 3; page 31).

I should note that the non-profit organization, Dayton Police History Foundation, Inc., motivates all research that is conducted on local law enforcement and garners warm support. Several descendents of Dayton police officers have contributed selflessly to the efforts of DPH Foundation and, in so doing, this book:

Carolyn J. Burns, granddaughter of Patrolman Frank W. Johnson (1902-1936); **Tom Grundish**, grandson of Dayton Police Inspector Thomas C. Grundish (1905-1934); retired St. Petersburg (Fla) Police Officer **Dave Klippel**, great-grandson of Captain Edward F. Poland (1910-1935); and **Jack Barstow,** grandson of Dayton Police Chief Rudolph F. Wurstner (1902-1949).

The photo images of Patrolman Grundish and Patrolman Wurstner appear in the story in Part 4, pages 59 and 61 respectively.

Patrolman Johnson

Patrolman Poland

Carolyn contributed a number of police photographs that appear herein. The image of the battered brass-colored badge that appears in the Prologue belonged to Tom's grandfather. Dave provided research and donated copies of his grandfather's scrapbook and journal; and Jack often provides background on his grandfather that would not otherwise be known.

The Honorable Judge **Daniel Gehres** made available a letter written by one of his relatives, Amos Crow, who survived the 1913 Flood.

Retired Dayton Police Lieutenant **Michael Sammons** (1960-1991) offered his assistance when I believed I most needed it in preparing for this edition of *Drenched Uniforms and Batter Badges*. His thorough review and spot-on suggestions improved the readability of the book.

Mary Oliver and **Gwenyth Haney**, the collections administrators for Dayton History at Carillon Historical Park, always offer assistance with every project I undertake. Mary has a soft spot for law enforcement; her father, Edward Duffy, was an Ohio State Highway Patrol trooper. Gwen, a persistent researcher, enthusiastically calls whenever she comes across any photo or tidbit of information related to local policing.

Lastly, ***Dayton History Books Online*** has featured a number of my stories over the past four years, fostering the improvement of my writing skills over time.

Thank you all.

The Great Dayton Flood of 1913

Floodwaters surging at the Dayton View Bridge

Deep Waters Flood South Ludlow Street

Dayton police wagon drivers and jail turnkeys (Ptl. Frank Johnson, second from right)
Courtesy of Carolyn J Burns, granddaughter of Ptl. Johnson

Table of Contents

Introduction
A Face to the Name
11

Prologue
Drenched Uniforms and Battered Badges
15

Part 1
Police Readiness
17

Part 2
Flood Forecasts
23

Part 3
Breached Levees
31

Part 4
Loss of Life
53

Part 5
Military Protection
65

Epilogue
1913 - 1922
85

Endnotes
103

Introduction

A Face to the Name

The 100-year anniversary of one of the nation's worst natural disasters is not an event to be celebrated but – because of the people who rose to the challenges brought on by adversity – is one to be recalled with pride and reflection. Throughout 2013, the story of the Great Dayton Flood will be recounted often and in many ways. As a retired Dayton police sergeant, I wanted this narrative to be told from a law enforcement perspective but with an added component... I wanted the faces of the officers who endured this dreadful episode in our local history to be seen.

The city of Dayton outfits its officers in blue uniforms with polished badges so they will be instantly recognizable to the public; but uniformity in dress also tends to lump officers together in a way that makes them faceless to the citizenry they protect.

I was reminded of this in 2006 when I attended the National Law Enforcement Officers Memorial ceremony in Washington, D.C. Tragically, 24 Dayton police officers have sacrificed their lives since 1880 in service to their community and were forever lost to their families. In searching for the engraved names on the granite wall, I sadly discovered that four were misspelled. In checking a national website dedicated to the memories of the "fallen" officers, I found only four pictured. What did the other 20 officers look like? I wanted to see the faces of our slain heroes. Since then, the four names have been accurately inscribed on the memorial wall and the photographs of all but two – Ptl. Lee Lynam (1880) and Ptl. William "Tom" Wilson (1928) – have been located and posted online.

That experience remains a constant personal reminder that, whenever possible, photo images of our officers should accompany any story I write about local law enforcement... there must be a face to the name.

Readers will find well over 20 photographs of Dayton police officers in *Drenched Uniforms and Battered Badges*. The story is a tribute to the 1913 heroes in blue. This rendering of the Great Dayton Flood is a compilation of many period news reports and other source materials; none did more than scratch the surface on the true measure of these Dayton patrolmen. I assembled passages from these scant accounts to mold an amalgamated narrative on the role of Dayton law enforcement during the catastrophe's rescue and relief efforts.

Rather than abandon their posts to safeguard their families, homes, and property, patrolmen regrettably forsook their wives and children so as to aid the terrified and helpless in our local community. The officers' troubled families had to fend for themselves. Not only did the police act with selfless resolve during the first three treacherous, anxiety-filled days, they continued to press forward with little rest, under miserable conditions over the following weeks.

On April 14, 1913, the Dayton Daily News proclaimed that the public safety officers' "remarkable work of rescue [during the flood] ..., while their own families were suffering, will never be forgotten." The truth is their remarkable work has not been remembered.

This book is my way to capture and preserve their noteworthy efforts. All members of the 1913 Dayton police force sacrificed for their community. I wish I could show and name them all.

"In Valor There is Hope"
National Law Enforcement Officers Memorial

Patrolman William Dalton (foreground) killed in the line of duty in 1899

The Dayton Mounted Patrol Unit escorts the riderless horse to
Officer William 'Steve' Whalen's gravesite service in 1991

Drenched Uniforms and Battered Badges – Prologue

A community looks to its police force and its fire department whenever there is risk to loss of life and property. The safety services come to the aid of the citizens they are sworn to protect when tragedy strikes; but when a natural disaster of the enormity of the "Great Dayton Flood" abruptly and rapidly overtakes a city of 120,000 people, the first responders – the police – are in the same way besieged.

This was sadly the case in 1913.

Dayton Police Headquarters (2nd floor) at South Main & Market Streets; police entrance (left). Today, the location of the Greater Dayton RTA central hub.

Part 1

Police Readiness

Dayton police patrolman; pristine **police uniform** circa 1913
Off. Derric D. McDonald; *photograph by Off. Amy M. Simpson*

Police Readiness

Law enforcement in Dayton had not changed much from the day in 1833 when the first watchman, Joseph L. Allen, was appointed by the town marshal to patrol a designated square downtown. [1,2] Dayton patrolmen of 1913 sauntered paths on worn shoe leather to protect the citizens on their police beats. These men made their rounds 12 or more hours every day with only one day off every two weeks. Exactly 40 years earlier in 1873, the *Dayton Metropolitan Police Force* was established. Just as then, patrolmen in 1913 carried 'pocket pistols' beneath outer coats, J. Hudson whistles in another pocket and a hickory night stick swinging from a leather strap around their wrists. Patrolmen wore the rounded 'London bobby'-style hat which afforded greater height so as to be seen by citizens seeking help.

Patrol Station No. 1 on Brown Street at E. Fifth Street

Only 30 years earlier in 1883 the police force acquired its first horse-drawn patrol wagon. Horses were few and valued in police service. In 1893 a mounted patrol unit, comprised of eight patrolmen and a sergeant, began making the rounds of the neighborhoods. The number of mounted officers would never increase. The police force operated the ambulance service (continuing that practice until 1950). A horse-drawn ambulance and two horse wagons were the entirety of the police fleet in 1903, the year the Wright brothers achieved powered-flight and only 10 years before the Great Flood.

Motorized travel was new to the general public in 1903 and slow in coming to the Dayton police force. Only two years before the flood had the police even begun to modernize.

In 1911, the city purchased four motorcycles and assigned two each to the outlying precincts. [3:4] By 1913, the police motorcycle squad was replacing mounted officers. Predictably, it was comprised of eight 'motor cops' and a sergeant, the exact composition of the vanishing mounted patrol unit.

In 1912, the Dayton police force acquired its first motorized "Department of Public Safety" utilitarian wagon. It was the start toward the end of horse-drawn ambulance and prisoner wagons. The acquisition of a single police automobile, a Model T Ford, was still three years in the future.

Aside from the mechanics of patrol, the Dayton Police Department has a history that continues to this day of being understaffed relative to its local crime rate and to other police departments of equal constitution. In the four years on either side of 1913, the Dayton force maintained an 'authorized strength' of 160 sworn officers and 11 civilian employees. [5:6] But the year 1913 began with financial conditions worse than at any time since the outset of the new century.

The 1893 Panic had placed the city in a slow recovery from an economic depression that lasted over a decade. Then, on January 21, 1913, the police force again cut its manpower, [7] and this time by a full 15%. There were 24 officers dismissed from service because of a "shortage of funds." [8]

And so it was at the opening to the year that an ill-equipped police force was first hampered with a severe reduction in ranks leading into its encounter with the worst natural disaster in the city's history of floods, recorded in 1805, 1814, 1828, 1847, 1866, 1883 and 1886. The episodic, serious breaches of the banks and levees were not faded memories. The high and compromising water cascades in the month of March were as recent as 15 years earlier: 1897 closely followed once more in 1898. [9]

The experience from these more recent episodes was flood waters as high as *two feet* in the low-lying areas; enough damage and difficulties to call for the repeated shoring up of the levees but no long-term plan in preparation for the next calamity… one, as it turns out, that would result in the worst in human suffering and property destruction. In 1913 the future became the present but, at the onset, was seemingly no different than the past.

Police Assembly at Dayton police **Patrol House** on Sears Street

By any measure, the Dayton police force was undermanned, under-equipped and, after March 24, 1913, underwater and overwhelmed.

Part 2

Flood Forecasts

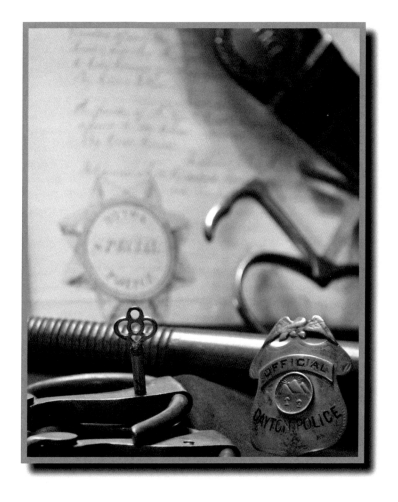

Dayton police badge, ledger, handcuffs, baton, belt, nipper
Photograph by Off. Amy M. Simpson

Flood Forecasts

At 11:30 a.m. on Monday, March 24, Harry Alps of the United States Weather Bureau telephoned Albert Mays Dodds, Dayton's director of public safety. Alps advised him to expect relatively serious flooding in some of the residential areas and maybe *a few inches* on the downtown streets: "The official flood stage is eighteen feet but the levees should be able to contain up to twenty-three feet." [10] Director Mays Dodds notified his two superintendents – Police Chief John N. Allaback and Fire Chief Frank B. Ramby – of the storm's likely consequence.

Five hours later, however, Alps telephoned Dodds with an update. He advised at 4:45 p.m. that matters would be much worse and suggested the public safety director consider what they had discussed earlier in the day; that the National Guard be called so it could be prepared for an emergency response. [11] Soon thereafter, Police Chief Allaback learned that the "lowland" would experience more severe flooding than first thought and that some other places might sustain an unexpected overflow. Even though he believed his on-duty personnel could handle the circumstances associated with the weather, he directed the police central exchange operator to call every off-duty officer and place them on stand-by notice until further advised.

Police Chief Allaback

Chief Allaback, a 27-year veteran, instructed his assistant to have patrolmen pulled from their beats in the outlying police precincts and deployed to the central city neighborhoods most vulnerable to high water. Flooding was a recurring problem in the spring and this practice was not unusual. It was standard operating procedure to alert the residents in specific neighborhoods to vacate to safer places. On this evening, patrolmen were directed to go "house-to-house in North Dayton, the near West Side, Riverdale, lower Dayton View and all the other areas near the levees to warn the residents and advise them to leave for higher ground immediately." [12]

The warnings Chief Allaback received from the national weather service earlier in the evening became reality at midnight. The East Herman Avenue levee began to weaken from the intensity of the Great Miami River swell. The Dayton police force, having been notified of this development, began to sound the "warning sirens and alarms". [13]

At 2:20 a.m. on Tuesday, March 25, Harry Alps again called Safety Director Dodds. He told him to anticipate flooding of at least *two feet* in the downtown area and *five* to *six feet* in the lower residential areas; neighborhoods like Riverdale. Dodds in turn called Chief Allaback with instructions to have his patrolmen hurriedly evacuate the neighborhoods that would most likely be affected. [14]

Sergeant Johnson   Sergeant Tupman

Patrolmen on both sides of town received orders from their sergeants who also assisted in hastily alerting citizens in danger. Sgt. William A. Johnson, a 17-year veteran, was patrolling in north Dayton and could see the fast-rising Mad River. Sgt. Homer L. Tupman, a 12-year veteran, witnessed the same on the west side at Wolf Creek.

These two tributaries, along with the Stillwater River, were bloated, rising and choked at their points of convergence ... the swollen and fiercely flowing Great Miami River. A tapering one-mile stretch between the Mad River and Wolf Creek divided the river's double bend. In that narrowing path, the Miami could not absorb the wicked torrent of three merging channels. Low lands to the north and east could expect to be overtaken by the perilous rush of flood waters.

Patrolman Jenkins

At 2:20 in the morning, Sgt. Tupman, in the company of Ptl. William R. Jenkins, a 15-year veteran and Dayton's first black police officer, walked door-to-door waking sleeping citizens residing along the Wolf Creek levee. At this unreasonable hour the officers implored families to move to high ground. By 4:00 o'clock, they were able to persuade nearly 200 families living on their beat of the urgency to abandon the comfort of their homes. "The streets were lively with people heading toward the hill [to the west toward Soldiers Home]. It was at about this time that the streets began filling with water. Within forty minutes the water was gushing from the occasional unclosed sewers as if they were fountains, and within an hour they were wading in at least twenty inches of water." [15]

Wolfcreek breaking over the levee at Edgewater Avenue (Dakota Street)

At that same time in the bitterly cold morning, the first call from a citizen regarding the rising river came into the police station. Andrew M. Fox, who lived at 629 N. Main Street, realized the pending danger an hour earlier and had loaded his wagon with household items. He and his wife were leaving home to go to a safer location but decided to find out what the police might know about the circumstances. He was told by the police operator that a flood was coming but Fox did not get a feeling that the officer to whom he spoke was particularly alarmed. [16]

By 5:30 in the morning, small detachments of soldiers and greater-than-typical numbers of police officers were moving about downtown. In the pouring rain, people crowded on the levees "watching the fascinating spectacle of over one hundred thousand cubic feet of water passing every second. On the levee along Monument Avenue there were literally hundreds of people, with the most congested area between Main Street and Monument Avenue" [17] near Dayton's main fire house.

Crowd forms at Dayton View Bridge north of Monument Street

Part 3

Breached Levees

Dayton police turnkey; tattered **police uniform** circa 1913
Off. Kyle A. Treon; *photograph by Off. Amy M. Simpson*

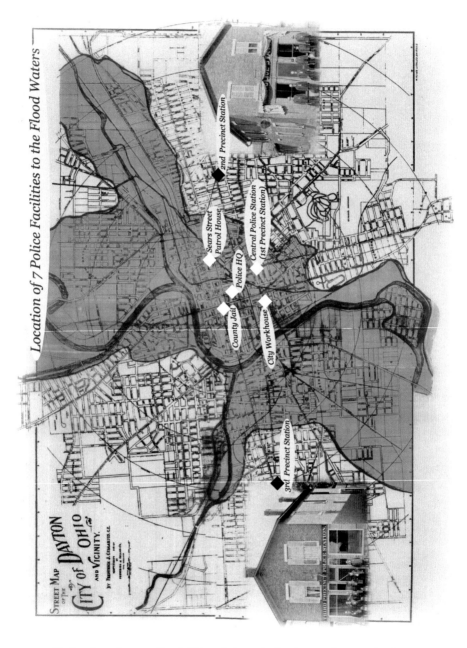

Location of 7 Police Facilities to the Flood Waters

2nd Precinct Station

Sears Street Patrol House

Police HQ

Central Police Station (1st Precinct Station)

County Jail

City Workhouse

3rd Precinct Station

STREET MAP OF THE CITY OF DAYTON OHIO AND VICINITY.
By Frederick J. Chandler, C.E.

The locations of seven police facilities relative to the flood waters; five overtaken by
the flood and two on higher grounds – the 2nd and 3rd Precinct Station Houses.

Breached Levees

Within the hour at 6:35 a.m., the view north was no longer just a curious site. The disaster-in-the-making ruptured into its full fury. The low ground of White City (now called Island Park) on the opposite side of the Helena Street bridge was submerged and, from that vantage point, "the expanse of flooding ... stretched as far as ... could [be seen] into North Dayton." [18] One mile further south, the Mad River was incapable of pouring its excess into the Great Miami River. Dayton police Sgt. William Johnson was still in the area of the Keowee Street Bridge, which spanned the Mad River. On the downtown south side of the bridge was the Miami-Erie Canal that paralleled through the plants of the Barney & Smith Car Company, a world-wide producer of elegant railroad cars. To the north were hundreds of people who lived in the ethnic neighborhoods of Polish, Hungarian and Lithuanian immigrants.

Riverdale looking east across the Great Miami River toward Mad River

"The pressure increased until the levee exploded. When the Mad River levee broke, the water burst forward five to 10 feet high upon shocked citizens. The water was 30° to 35°." [19] Sgt. Johnson did all he could to help those who had remained behind: "I can only tell you what I saw and, my God, that was bad enough. I saw women and children struggling in the water. Some were equal to the occasion but others were swept away and soon lost sight of. It was simply impossible to count them, so quickly was it done." [20]

On the other side of town Ptl. Jenkins and Sgt. Tupman were soon to experience the same. At 6:50 a.m. the Wolf Creek levee broke and both officers were suddenly swept away in a barrage of water. "They ran west in the middle of Cedar Street ... but they'd hardly gone a quarter of a block when the six-foot avalanche of water smashed into them, bowling them over and carrying them along nearly twice as fast as they'd been running." [21 : 22]

Men high on telephone wires to cross above flood waters

The two officers were separated by the flood and they found themselves frantically struggling to survive from drowning or being battered to death by the heavy debris churning in the cascading water. Both patrolmen managed to escape by latching onto trees and pulling themselves "over the water. They climbed to the top, where cables dipped through the branches midway between two telegraph poles, and from here they swung themselves hand over hand to the first pole and then walked along the wires for four blocks before reaching dry ground where they could alight and continue their work." [23]

Only 12 hours earlier, Chief Allaback had taken the precaution of redeploying the majority of his officers from the 2nd Precinct Station and the 3rd Precinct Station – East Third Street at

Linden Avenue and West Third Street near Grosvenor Avnue respectively – closer to the river levees near the center of town. Daily, two-thirds of Dayton patrolmen protected the community during the darkness of night. The night shift was from 6:00 in the evening to 6:00 in the morning, augmented by a cross-over shift of officers until midnight that could be drawn upon when emergencies surfaced. This was such an emergency. In the early morning hours of Tuesday, March 25, 1913 most Dayton patrolmen were positioned in proximity to downtown.

The *Central Police Station*, also known as the 1st Precinct, housed the city jail and police court. It was located on East Sixth Street near Tecumseh Avenue (in today's Oregon District). The *Patrol House* that held the ambulance, four wagons, a boat wagon and stable for 17 horses was located on Sears Street between North and South Ford Streets. These two primary police facilities were trapped in the flood plain. As a precaution, "the patrol wagons and ambulance were kept in the street at police headquarters [downtown to be] … dispatched from there." [24]

Dayton Police Headquarters: 1st floor underwater (4th building from right)

City Hall and *Dayton Police Headquarters* were located on the second floor of the Market House downtown. Only four blocks from the Great Miami River at 22 South Main Street (today the location of the Greater Dayton RTA central hub), this was the central office of the police chief, police commanders, detectives and central telephone exchange. Consequently, at the time of greatest crisis, the police facilities and sworn personnel were in the threat area, just as exposed to the ravages of flood as the citizenry it was obligated to protect.

It was from police headquarters on the morning of March 25 that Chief Allaback had initially directed his troops and would later prepare rescue operations ... except the Dayton chief of police now found he was "isolated" from his men. Allaback "was as powerless as his scattered patrolmen – all of whom were involuntarily on 'fixed posts' for the next forty-eight hours. Waterworks, telephones, electric lights, gas [and] every form of transportation – all had suddenly ceased to exist." [25]   Many of his officers now shared a common hardship with their fellow citizens. "Nearly one-third of the policemen and firemen lived in the downtown sections and [they, too,] lost nearly everything they had." [26]   The city safety services had "so many members who suffered the entire loss of [their] property... [that they were] absolutely destitute." [27]   They were victims also.

Dayton native and Army General George H. Wood had intended to travel to Columbus on Tuesday morning. Having risen early to observe the disaster advancing, he instead made a crucial decision: "The situation was critical, as all civil government had disappeared, and ... I assumed responsibility and declared Martial Law." [28]   This action was taken two days before another Daytonian and Dayton Daily News publisher, Ohio Governor James M. Cox, officially proclaimed a state of emergency.

Patrolmen, "scattered" on their foot beats, could maintain contact with police headquarters for a short time by relying on the Gamewell system – telephone *patrol call boxes* mounted on at least 64 poles throughout the city. Under normal conditions, the routine for patrolmen was to call the central exchange every hour to report in and receive instructions. Conversely, the central exchange was able to alert officers to check in from a call box if an emergency surfaced by illuminating red lights strategically suspended high above the city streets. It had been a dependable network since installed in 1896 and enhanced in 1902. During this catastrophe, "the entire Gamewell system [would be] the last line of communications to go out of service," [29] but in due course it also faltered in the icy waters. Officers were forced to act on their own instincts, particularly in the early stages of the staggering tragedy.

At 7:45 a.m. the overwhelmed police force was in urgent need of assistance from army troops. Sgt. Edwin S. Fair, a 36-year police veteran and most senior police supervisor with  26 years experience, was able to contact General Wood. Until then no other "Civil Authorities" had been in touch with the general. The sergeant asked General Wood to send soldiers to collect the boats from the boathouses at Y.M.C.A. Park (north of Ridge Avenue) and White City (i.e. Island Park), both on the west side of Stillwater Avenue (now Riverside Drive)

Sergeant Fair

north along the levee. The army general sent a detachment of men from the Third Infantry, G and K Companies. Soon after, at about 8:00 a.m., a detachment from the Ninth Infantry, Company C (Xenia) was ordered to go to North Dayton to assist Sgt. William Johnson and the burdened police at the Keowee Street Bridge. [30]

The flood waters were rising quickly and gushing turbulently. On the first day, the Ohio National Guard was not yet in sufficient numbers to coordinate rescue operations although the few soldiers in the field took lifesaving actions when needed. Many citizens also acted selflessly to save others.

The breached levee waters swallow North Dayton

Patrolman (far right) and fireman (center) on rope line (unidentified location)

Officers, such as 22-year veteran Ptl. Thomas Mitchell, were left to their devises and chose to work in partnership with citizens. In order to extricate people from homes and scenes of immediate risk, ropes were securely fastened around poles or trees and stretched across expanses of churning water. The current was so powerful that any attempt to cross streets to areas of safety without hold of a rope line was to invite

Patrolman Mitchell

being pulled underwater. Tupman and Ptl. Jenkins alone "saved 40 persons in small houses on Cedar Street by means of ropes." [31]

Others in the safety services did all they could to rescue people trapped in their homes. A 19-year fire veteran, Edward Doudna, was stationed at Hose Company No. 9 at 234 River

Fireman Doudna

Street (today Riverview Terrace between Salem Avenue and Dayton Street) when flood waters suddenly overpowered the neighborhood, rising to above the first story of homes. At 1:30 in the afternoon, Fireman Doudna was in a boat near 918 West Third Street (across from Sweetman Street). He maneuvered to the framed home to help

38

a woman escape through a second-story window. Stepping into the boat, she stumbled hard causing the standing fireman to lose his balance. "He fell into the swift current …. came up and tried to grab the boat but his heavy coat and boots weighted him down. He disappeared under the water." [32]

Rescue boat on Burns and Caroline Streets; black patrolman (far right); fireman (center)

Only three blocks southwest, a police officer, Ptl. Newton H. Haywood "waded into deep water and carried away many persons from their homes … [and] also carried many to a wagon … until the water became so deep there was danger of the horse swimming away." The patrolman, who lived on Hawthorn and Fourth Streets, was doing "a yeoman service rescuing his neighbors." He helped Bishop Milton Wright, father of the Wright brothers, and a lady next door from their homes into a boat for a "perilous journey of several blocks in a swift current." [33] The press reported that Ptl. Haywood aided Orville Wright and his sister Katharine, living at 7 Hawthorn Street, to a wagon allowing the family to reunite that day.

Patrolman Haywood

The continuous deluge in North Dayton was such that the Barney & Smith plants were awash "in *12 feet* of water." Other neighborhoods would be submerged in even deeper water. There were reports that northwest across the Great Miami River "in Riverdale and Dayton View, water rose as high as *20 feet*." [34]   In the lower sections of Riverdale, people were being rescued from their homes in unsteady boats taken from the Riverdale canoe club.

Flood waters overtaking Riverdale neighborhood at McDaniel Street

At Geyer and Warder Streets, bundled twin babies were seen in the water as people screamed in horror from second story homes. The baby boy "had gone down, sucked under by a whirlpool at the junction of the two streets ..." while the twin girl was adrift "in the current straight down Warder street towards the river ...." [*sic*] Each was saved when pulled into separate boats. The twin boy was "delivered to a policeman who had recently finished a course of first aid given at the Y.M.C.A." He rubbed and warmed the soaked child. After an hour the patrolman saw "the first signs of returning life. The blue face became white, the blackened lips took on their normal hue and by the time the mother appeared on the scene both children were on their way to complete recovery." [35]

There were other acts of heroism by police and fire as well as National Guardsmen. They maneuvered in water that was "shoulder deep" to fasten ropes to establish a "safe port" in the lower section of Riverdale across Main Street.

Citizens on rope line with policeman (right) and fireman (center)
From the Dayton History Collection

"Two men in a boat pushed under the rope, were caught by the current and swept ... into the main channel of the river. One never appeared again; the other caught in the branches of a tree about twenty-five feet south of the bridge. Two most heroic attempts were made by officers and soldiers ... to rescue this man, but both failed. In the second attempt Battalion Sergeant Major Edward L. Harper, Third Ohio Infantry, lost his life." [36]

Patrolman McGovern   Patrolman Altherr

Despite being "disorganized by lack of communication," individual members of the police department repeatedly placed themselves in harm's way to perform "hundreds of heroic deeds" in all parts of town. On the south edge of the canal running diagonally through Dayton, rescue efforts by Ptl. Frank McGovern and Ptl. George L. Altherr "stand out." The officers were east of the Central Police Station on Tuesday morning traveling to higher ground in their ambulance when they came across women and children in danger at Wayne Avenue and State Street. The patrolmen carried many of them in chest-deep water to the second floor of the Courier automobile plant. The officers then "chopped a hole in the floor and rescued Firemen Raffles and Stuck (believed to be Dayton firemen Albert A. Raffle and Edward W. Stock), who were imprisoned on the first floor." [37] [*sic*]

The Courier plant became the safe haven for 385 citizens living in nearby homes. Patrolmen Altherr and McGovern remained with the stranded people over the course of the two days (until Thursday dawn) and "maintained order" at the plant. Together with the firemen and police court judge William Budroe, "who doubtless owed his life" to the officers, they cared for the refugees. "There was little food – far from enough to supply all. The building was threatened by fire in the vicinity, but the flames did not reach it." [38] The officers were able to obtain some food and evenly divide it.

Although cold, people were prevented from starting fires. "The action of the ambulance crew in sticking to the work of rescue of imperiled persons caused a final wrecking of the vehicle which they drove." [39] The police force could hardly afford to lose one of the few vehicles it had.

Overlooking East Dayton from Miami Valley Hospital high ground

In the absence of coordinated police and fire emergency response, the most influential private citizen in Dayton, John H. Patterson, the owner of National Cash Register Company (N.C.R.), began to take action early Tuesday. At first it was for self-preservation. Patterson had 50 men chosen from among his foremen to act as an unarmed auxiliary police force and fire brigade, initially to conduct patrol around his industrial plant in south Dayton. He wanted his facility secured and safe from rioting, theft and fire. [40] But the necessity for engaging citizens in policing efforts would expand beyond the confines of the plant grounds later this day.

By Tuesday afternoon, General Wood met with the Public Safety Director Dodds. In an effort to suppress the anticipated looting and lawlessness in the community at large that happens when homes and businesses are vacated, "volunteer guards, special deputies, and citizen police [were] sworn in as such ...." [41]

N.C.R. view of swollen Great Miami River; Stewart Street bridge (upper right)

In the meantime, Dayton Mayor Edward Philipps met with John Patterson, the man who would take the civilian lead in the recovery efforts. Patterson had already instructed N.C.R. foremen to have nearly 300 flat-bottomed boats constructed for rescue teams, and they were placed in use upon completion. By 1:00 Tuesday afternoon, Mayor Philipps declared N.C.R.

to be the emergency operation center for police, fire, military and medical personnel. [42]   It became the base for providing food, shelter and medical care to thousands of stranded citizens. Many members from the wider Dayton community would later volunteer to help in the relief efforts.

Relief boat delivering supplies to St. Elizabeth Hospital

In the midst of the rescue efforts directed from N.C.R. – and compounding the fears that came with the unexpected horrors of reality – there was intensifying anxiety about a looming threat. Staring from the Fairgrounds in "the cold and snow in the early morning", a woman wrote in her diary, she could see the devastation of the flood. She penned, "[We] saw men rescuing people in boats everywhere [but] on our return [home] we were met with cries of 'To the hill, the water is coming' and people running. I got my children, … and started for the hill … there was a steady stream of people going up the hill carrying babies, bundles of every description, automobile loads, wagon loads, buggies, horses, heavy wagons, people with quilts around them, sick people being carried and hauled, hysterical women, ... myself included." [43]

Terrifying rumors rapidly circulated. Millions of gallons of water from a collapsed 13,000 acre Lewiston Reservoir (today Indian Lake) were surging toward a city already under 16 feet of water in some districts. This "news" was causing a general panic throughout the Miami Valley corridor as far south as Hamilton,

Ohio: "Run … [a] wall of water [is] rushing down river!" [44]

Lewiston was one of three reservoirs north of Dayton that served the Miami-Erie Canal (the other two being today's Lake Loramie and Grand Lake St. Marys). It was the largest of the group and only 60 miles from Dayton. The terror that a "wall of water" was rushing down the Great Miami River was, as later learned, utterly without merit but not an irrational dread. [45]

Patrolman with N.C.R. motor car and "No Need For Alarm" sign

In an effort to quash the gripping fears of the community, officers such as 10-year veteran Ptl. Charles R. Wilkins - the longest-serving officer in Dayton history (1903-50) - were dispatched in N.C.R. automobiles with signs that read:

"No Need for Alarm - Lewiston Reservoir Did Not Break." [46]

Patrolman Wilkins

Even though the Lewiston scare was untrue, devastation continued unabated for two solid days. Downtown restaurant owner and flood survivor, Amos Crow, would later express in a letter his disbelief at all he was witnessing and experiencing, "People climbed up in trees and stayed there for 48 hours in all that rain and sleet with out shelter or drink. The water was 13 ft deep on the restaurant floor the ceiling is 14 ft and it struck up on the joice about 3 inches. I saw houses go down the river and people on top of them. [We] lost the wholesale place and the restaurant the walls all washed away from the building we were in." [47] [*sic*]

Another flood survivor, Harry Rogers, recalled, "The water rose and rose with almost incredible speed and ... it was obvious that the situation was really serious. By early afternoon ... the current was rushing by at a tremendous speed carrying with it trees, fences, small buildings, and, worst of all, horse after horse frantically swimming and screaming." [48] People were hollering from all quarters for help and those lucky enough to be in earshot of a "hastily improvised boat" constructed at the N.C.R. plants were rescued. "All night long the water roared and the horses [shrieked] and shouts for help could be heard." [49] The human suffering was distressing but the toll on animals "was haunting. Horses struggled for hours whinnying and snorting looking for dry ground but succumbing to the icy cold water." [50]

Horses struggling in churning flood waters downtown

The river level reached 24 feet on Tuesday. On the second day, Wednesday, March 26, the situation worsened as the river reached its highest level at 28.1 feet. [51] And when the surge subsided, the water reversed course but even then, the calm that came did not instantly evaporate the "4 trillion gallons" [52] of high waters and dangerous conditions.

Neighborhood homes partially submerged in high waters (unidentified location)

Later that day, as the waters finally and slowly began to recede, a natural gas vein ruptured in a downtown business; the shut-off valve was 15 feet underwater. The gas line exploded in fire with flames blazing upwards of 50 feet high. The worst fires were to structures north of West Third Street and then sparked across the street to the Lowe Brothers Paint Company. Nearly two entire central city blocks were consumed. Now known as the "Fire Blocks," buildings between St. Clair and Jefferson Streets, and Second and Fourth Streets, were reduced to ashes and charred-brick shells.

Lowe Brothers Paint Store in the 'Fire Blocks' at East Third and Jefferson Streets

On the third day, Thursday, March 27, the river level decreased to 22.2 feet. Dayton police officers worked tirelessly hour-after-hour during the first two to three days to assist as many citizens in harms way as they possibly could. And throughout the hours and the days that followed, they themselves were in constant injurious jeopardy from flood waters, exposure, and floating, falling or hidden debris ... officers such as Ptl. Pete Hunter, who was badly hurt, but narrowly "escaped from death" when a large plank used as a building brace broke free and "missed his head by only a few inches ....;" [53] Ptl. Howard Hunter, injured by a floating log during high waters; Ptl. Charles L. Kurfiss painfully wounded from a nail protruding in the debris; and Ptl. James Conway, who suffered chest congestion from the elements. [54] The 42-year old Ptl. Conway survived the flood but, sadly and to his fellow officers' disbelief, died on February 20, 1914 after battling a chronic and "virulent malady" for nearly a year. [55 : 56]

Patrolman H. Hunter   Patrolman Kurfiss   Patrolman Conway

By Thursday the dynamics of the catastrophe began to refocus from "search and rescue" activities to "recovery," security, and relief operations. As the flood waters retreated to the rivers, General Wood was able to assert martial law in dry areas in districts established by military staff. "By night fall, the water had receded to the southern line of Third Street, but every inch of fall meant additional guard duty as every store and bank door had been forced open by the elements and their contents lay open to any marauder." [57]

Early Friday morning, the people who had been stranded in downtown businesses, shops and apartments since Tuesday were finally able to emerge from their isolating but protective shelters. "They were directed to keep off the sidewalks and travel in the middle of the streets and were directed [south toward N.C.R.] and assisted to places of safety." [58]

N.C.R. rescue boats on East Fifth Street at Bomberger Park

It had been four days since that ill-fated Monday morning when Harry Alps of the U.S. Weather Bureau, as a matter of course, telephoned with his report of potential flooding – "maybe a few inches" – on the downtown streets of Dayton. Thereafter, under rapidly worsening conditions and without direction, patrolmen stood fast on their beats enduring a most ruthless facet of nature – ice cold rain. It bucketed on top of them and swelled upon the frozen ground with suddenness never before experienced – over their shoes to their shins, then thighs and frighteningly higher.

Receding waters, East First Street looking west; Barney & Smith Company plants

49

Miserable to the core, wool coats saturated and heavy, police officers persisted in their mission to rescue and comfort those in desperate need. The near-freezing air penetrated drenched uniforms, chilling clammy flesh. The elements relentlessly battered their tired and aching bodies.

Few patrolmen took leave to see to the safety of their families, eat a decent meal, bathe, change clothes or get sufficient sleep. And when the leather soles of their shoes had dried, they vigilantly remained on 24-hour protective watch for more days to come.

Patrolmen would not relinquish their beats until certain that the urgent nature of this terrible catastrophe had abated.

The flood's aftermath on East First Street

The early efforts of Dayton's public safety officers did not go unnoticed or unappreciated in the community. "It was the policemen and firemen who first warned Daytonians of their danger, and it was they who were the last to seek refuge when waters got beyond their strength and depth .... They worked like Trojans.

Yet when the waters had receded they did not rest. Many worked themselves sick ... yet, as soon as they were able they again went back to their respective lines, and ... hold themselves in readiness to meet any emergency." [59]

The frantic rescue activities were over; the recovery was beginning. Chief Allaback, "himself marooned" [60] at police headquarters, was able to provide leadership to the men from whom he had been separated for days.

After learning of their fate, the chief's first order of business was to have his officers search for trapped survivors...

... and the dead.

Part 4

Loss of Life

Horse-drawn Dayton **police ambulance**; driver Ptl. Frank Johnson
Courtesy of Carolyn J. Burns, granddaughter of Ptl. Johnson

Loss of Life

The three days of near annihilation had ended; many days of anguish lay ahead.

The three Dayton newspapers – The Dayton Daily News, The Dayton Journal, and The Dayton Evening Herald – had been victims of the flood and fire. The only local information came from Dayton Daily News bulletins issued from the offices of N.C.R. or through word of mouth. The reliability of the latter method was evidenced by the Lewiston reservoir scare. The local newspapers were a week away from publishing again. The flood scene was off limits to all but authorized personnel, and the inaccessibility applied to reporters. So, a speculative press from New York to Alaska in a tabloid age of coverage brought the "facts" to the national public.

"Dayton is in Flames" (Newark Advocate);
"Flames Menace Dayton; Hundreds Flee"; (New York Journal);
"More Dams Break in Flood"; (New York Journal);
"Flood Spreading; Death List Grows" (Fairbanks Daily Times);
"Staggering Holocaust in Dayton" (Modesto Evening News);
"5000 Believed Dead" (Wichita Daily Times). [61]

Catherine Street homes submerged in South Dayton

The national news was reporting up to 10,000 people having died. The number of deaths would be bad enough; the truth revealed substantially less. The actual figure needed to be determined by the police and communicated as quickly as possible. Chief Allaback, having been isolated for two days, began checking on the whereabouts of community leaders. Certain parts of the city were virtually impassable.

Dayton Mayor Edward Philipps lived at 37 South Mound Street, between where Bishop Wright was rescued and where Fireman Doudna drowned. He was among the missing on Friday. The chief "had been unable to get near the Philipps house and did not know whether [the mayor] would be found dead or alive." [62] As it turned out, he had indeed survived but his experience was harrowing when the flood level reached "17 feet" at his house. "The water drove them to the second floor, and at high water mark was within one inch of the ceiling of the upstairs rooms. As the water came higher, a hole was punched through the ceiling and the family climbed into the attic, remaining there until rescued ...." [63]

Patrolman (far left); John H. Patterson (center wearing derby)

By Friday, Chief Allaback had received enough information from his men to offer a more rational estimate to the press, significantly reducing the speculative number of fatalities. Having checked on residents on the south side, Chief Allaback related, "Except for possible loss of life on the north side of the river there will not be more than 200 dead in Dayton ..." [64] Later, Chief Allaback was able to inform the correspondent for the Associated Press that the number of dead from the devastation of the flood was considerably fewer than the 200 he had put forward. Patrolmen and soldiers were able to "penetrate" North Dayton "where the topography of the land is more dangerous" than any other area of town.

The national news was able to report: "As nearly as can be ascertained about 100 persons were drowned in Riverdale, the first section of the city to be flooded. The rushing waters overturned several houses there and rolled them over and over with their occupants inside." The chief advised that the number of dead in East Dayton and Dayton View was small. [65] Even with police estimates, local citizens seeing the recovered bodies and speaking aloud still speculated that the number of dead was higher. One man wrote to his out-of-town relatives: "I do not think the dead will reach over (400) four hundred .... If it would came at night it would have been much worse. But it came early Tuesday morning ...." [66] [*sic*]

Bodies were found trapped inside houses and outside, anywhere the waters had turbulently flowed ... caught in the wreckage, floating in the rivers, washed up on the banks. The deaths were not restricted to the city. The appalling tally of flood-related fatalities throughout the state Ohio was "462 ... [of which] 98 souls perished in Dayton, the greatest number in any one city." [67] The numbers included Fireman Doudna and Army Sergeant Major Harper. No policeman died during the flood or in the immediate aftermath.

Debris in Riverdale on Shaw Avenue at McDaniel Street

Flood victim at Court House carried by citizens to central morgue

The grim task of gathering the remains of those who had perished was the first and foremost order of business. On Friday, March 28, John Patterson put out a call to all Dayton undertakers to meet with him at the N.C.R. emergency operation center at 8:00 in the evening. [68] A temporary morgue was set up at the N.C.R. garage but later moved to 217 West Third Street. Under "normal" emergency circumstances the responsibility for the removal of a dead body or few would fall to patrolmen manning the police ambulance or patrol wagons. Instead, this heartbreaking "undertaking" was handled by many in the community.

N.C.R. published edition of the Dayton Daily News Flood Extra

As with other citizens, patrolmen on duty and away from their families experienced the pain of distressing death notifications about their loved ones.

Catharine Grundish, diagnosed with pulmonary tuberculosis in December 1912, suffered from deteriorating health when the levees were breached. On Wednesday, March 26, the worst day of the flood, the young woman was examined by her doctor at her home (high ground in East Dayton at 62 South Van Lear Street). Her condition was bleak and yet her husband, Ptl. Thomas G. Grundish, could not be at her side. He was struggling with flood waters to protect lives. Three days later on March 29, Catharine Grundish died at age 37. [69] Her husband was still in the field assisting flood victims when told of her death. [70]

Patrolman Grundish

On that same day, Officer George A. Klinger, who was assigned to Union Station but drawn into duty at the central morgue, "received the news that his brother was a victim of the flood [when he] ... lost his life under falling walls in the uptown district." The officer was "compelled to abandon his post ... to confirm the report." [71]

In the last few days of March, before the local presses were operating, the only local published news came from the printing facility at N.C.R. Later, as the local newspapers returned to full production, the names of the missing, as conveyed by relatives and others, were printed in the daily news. Initially, reports on the dead were unreliable and there was also uncertainty as to the cause of death, be it flood, natural causes precipitated by the flood, or natural causes alone. As late as April 6, officials of the Red Cross society estimated the local death figure at 150. [72]

The human toll of the first four days, as well as the property destruction – "1,000 homes were damaged and destroyed" in the city – were harsh, traumatizing realities endured by the community but the loss of animal life was wretched; an incredible

"1,400 horses drowned along with many other animals." [73]

The horse carcasses were a miserable sight, only preserved from typical putrefaction by bitterly cold water and air. A postal telegram wired from one Daytonian to his nephew related: "Newspapers or your own imagination can not picture the horrors or sights one can witness ... the horses ... [a] poor old scout tried to get over the wagons but some cruel thing hit him in the side ...." [74]

A dead horse tangled in a guy wire along the railroad track

Another man wrote, "Our horses were drowned ... in a livery barn close to the wholesale house. There were about 100 horses in that barn ... [and] 27 of them never got out... died up on the stalls.... I saw one horse hanging up by the heals on a guy wire with just his head touching the ground." [75] [*sic*] The big animals were suspended in the steel girders of bridges, strewn in the streets, caught in wooden debris, hooked to wagons, tethered to posts, and twisted in downed pole wires ... the carnage from nature's ferocity.

Makley & Stomps Livery and Stables was typical of a local trade that experienced mass casualties to its boarded horses. The stable was located at 117-119 East Fourth Street on the southern end of the "Fire Blocks." It had "all but eight of their three hundred horses, many newly purchased, drowned in [flood] waters." [76] The massive loss between the flood and fire brought that livery business to an abrupt end in 1913.

A dead horse hanging from a steel bridge girder

Decomposing animals throughout the city, left unattended, would ensure the spread of cholera and typhoid fever. Removal became a vital, second order of business. A Friday morning bulletin issued from N.C.R. proclaimed: "Sanitation is a big problem. With care on the part of everyone, and quick, organized work, sickness may be avoided, impossible as it now seems." [77] The sludge, refuse, and wreckage needed to be disposed properly but nothing could create unsanitary conditions and bring disease faster than the massive animal remains strewed everywhere.

Members of the Dayton police force were initially assigned the repugnant duty of hauling away the animals. This was not uncommon as part of law enforcement service. This *police* task had been written in ordinance as early as 1826 when the town

Patrolman Wurstner

marshal was charged with removing "any dead animal or other offensive matter or substance ... in any of the streets, alleys, lots or commons...." [78]

Ptl. Rudy Wurstner – a man who would later become Dayton's longest-serving police chief in 1949 – was ordered to head up a detail responsible for the removal of horse carcasses from the city. His detail worked the area south of West Third Street, carting the animals six miles south to disposal grounds on the Great Miami River (near modern-day Moraine Air Park). The rescue and clean-up work was so demanding that Ptl. Wurstner, like his other fellow officers, "never made it home until a week after the flood." [79]

The military's attitude about unsanitary conditions was sterner than its warning to "sightseers" and equal to its stance on the threat of law breakers. A caution was printed in bold type on posted martial law declarations: "The strictest sanitary regulations will be enforced and citizens are requested to do their utmost to assist in this regard." And citizens did.

Horse carcasses alongside an overturned automobile

The Dayton Bicycle Club was one of the first to act. Many horse carcasses had been "taken to an island down river several miles below the city limits and burned." The bicycle club created 100 to 150 teams and, in doing so, relieved a nasty burden from police officers.

Beginning Saturday morning, March 29, these teams of men using "auto trucks" and railroad flat cars removed "1,250 dead horses, besides many dead dogs and cats" to Dayton and Xenia reduction plants. The work was completed within five days. [80] General Wood expressed his appreciation that the bicycle organization "volunteered to ... collect the carcasses and remove them to the fertilizing plant east of Dayton, and

… they performed this most disagreeable task in a business like and prompt manner." [81]

Horse carcasses on Ludlow Street at Second Street

While attending to the dead - both human and animal – a third order of business was carried out. Concentrated measures were underway to clean and rebuild the city. This could be done unimpeded only if peaceful conditions existed. Civil order was the authorized responsibility of soldiers inside the flood districts and the legal obligation of law enforcement officers now detailed to the outer perimeter.

Debris cleanup at Rikes Kumler on Second Street

Part 5

Military Protection

1913 declaration of **martial law** in Dayton, Ohio
From the Dayton History Collection

Military Protection

As of Friday, March 28, the city of Dayton was on deliberate lockdown; martial law was in full effect. The river level had dropped to 15.7 feet [82] and the fire department was back to being able to perform regular fire duties. This was a safety function best left to it than the military, which was more suited to security. Safeguarding and patrol were normal duties of the police but the areas of devastation open to human prey would require 18 times the personnel that this police force of 136 sworn officers could offer.

Flood Destruction at East Fifth Street and Mad River Road (now a Keowee Street Park)

By this fourth day, the central city and the designated adjacent districts came under the physical authority of 2,400 plus National Guard troops. Eventually, military headquarters was established at the Algonquin hotel, 11 South Ludlow Street (today the DoubleTree hotel). At the same time, the police department was "rapidly getting back into regulation harness and ... detailed to work in outlying sections." [83] Detectives remained downtown assigned to police headquarters. The areas beyond the flood district in the west-side 3rd Precinct and the east-side 2nd Precinct were in the hands of patrolmen and motor cops performing standard duties under the direction of sergeants. [84] Except for as-needed or menial assignments, routine security covering the city's interior was out of the jurisdiction of police and under the authority of military troops.

The reasons for the diminished police presence at the inner perimeter were obvious. The force did not have sufficient manpower, particularly having suffered itself during the worst of the catastrophe, and its infrastructure and facilities were out of commission, except for the two precinct offices. The *Central Police Station* on East Sixth Street, which housed the city jail, was badly damaged. In the immediate, this hampered normal police operations. In the long-term, the flood's wake was a blessing.

The United Brethren Church on East Sixth Street had been vacated 40 years earlier allowing the building to be acquired and converted into the Central Police Station. This was the first police facility when the department was organized in 1873. The physical condition of the station house, however, had been a source of complaints for a quarter of a century. The Board of Police Directors noted in its 1897-98 annual report that the police station was "condemned time and time again … [and was] unfit and dangerous for occupation." [85]

Central Police Station on East Sixth Street west of Tecumseh Street (flood debris along the curb) *From the NCR Archive at Dayton History*

A former police chief, Thomas Farrell, was blunt: "Words are not sufficient to describe its filth and deplorable condition. It is a disgrace to the city of Dayton or any civilized community."

He suggested the place be abandoned "in the interests of humanity and common decency." [86] In spite of that brutally frank assessment, 15 years later when the levees were breached, it was still in use.

Turnkey Dillman

Chief Farrell

Turnkey McMahon

The flood did what the politicians would not; the station would indeed be abandoned. "An examination made … showed that the cell block in the center of the main cell room is sinking. The foundation appeared to have been undermined." The public was reassured, however, that "all city prisoners are being lodged in jail with Turnkeys [Alonzo] Dillman and [Thomas] McMahon, of the police department, in charge." [87] The reassurance was necessary because the concerns were legitimate.

The "worst condition," as reported in the Washington Post, was at the *City Workhouse* on Friday when 60 prisoners threatened to revolt.

Prisoners inside the **City Workhouse** at South Main and West Sixth Streets
From the NCR Archive at Dayton History

The workhouse (formerly the old county jail) was located at South Main and West Sixth Streets. The inmates had not had food or water since Tuesday evening. They "demanded their liberty and a chance to fight for their lives." [88] The endangered warden had to threaten to shoot the prisoners if they attempted to escape. A detachment of soldiers was requested to help quell the revolt.

As men were arrested by Dayton police over the course of the next few weeks, they were incarcerated at the county jail behind the old court house on West Third Street instead of locked up in city cells.

In addition to the Central Police Station, the Sears Street Patrol House had been flooded with debris and the Gamewell communication system was inoperable.

Wrecked Dayton Department of Public Safety paddy wagon on South Main Street

The motorized police patrol wagon, which had been "safely" parked at police headquarters, was wrecked on South Main and Market Streets. The police discovered its "new automobile police patrol … [swept] through the flood just a few feet south of police headquarters, in front of the Baltimore dairy lunch room" [89] and Shroyer's Pool and Billiards hall. When the waters receded, the vehicle abutted a pole, the front had collision damage, and a whiskey barrel rested on its top.

Stranded citizens and float debris in flood waters (unidentified location)

Chief Allaback returned to directing his patrolmen in the outlying areas on Friday and to overseeing, as needed, law enforcement or other matters in the flood zones. The chief was also placed in charge of the citizens' relief committee. Its first act: "All grocery stores were commandeered and, although in most cases the goods were covered with water, … sufficient supplies were found to prevent great suffering among those in the interior dry strip." [90]

Flood refugees and refugee camp on riverbank

"Motorcycle relief squad"

Although "handicapped" by the flood, Dayton still had its full contingent of motorcycle officers. They proved to be the one available police resource able to contribute to the central city relief effort. The police force's nine motor cops were part of a 50-man "Motorcycle Relief Squad" that included private citizens.

"Making quick trips on their speedy machines and performing services which could never have been accomplished on foot, the motorcycle men [worked] incessantly since ... the day of the flood. Food, clothing and medicine were hurried to various points in emergency cases on the motorcycles, and while they were not otherwise engaged, the squad on the machines made excellent messengers ..." [91]

One of the distributions made in and outside Dayton were leaflets advising the public that martial law had been *ordered* by Governor Cox. The citizens of Dayton were asked to assist the National Guard troops numbering over 2,400. Sightseers and "excursionists" were not permitted in the city unless they could show "urgent business." Violators were warned that they would be "promptly arrested and confined ... [and] tried by the proper Military Tribunal. Thieves, looters and robbers [would] be dealt with summarily."

The nine Dayton police 'motor cops'

In addition to heeding to this military set of laws, people were *asked* to stay in their homes if at all possible but they were *required* to remain inside at certain hours. Signs were posted throughout the city that stated unconditionally "To the Citizens of Dayton: CURFEW will be sounded at 6:00 p.m. by the church bells. All citizens must keep off the streets from that time until 5:00 a.m. GEO. H. WOOD, Brig.-Gen. Com."

Curfew notice attached to wooden crate on Dayton bridge
From the Dayton History Collection

By Monday, March 31, a standard of conduct had been established for the citizenry of Dayton and understood. Even though the relief and cleanup efforts were the primary focus

of the community, there were those who found time to voice objections to the new restrictions. Local newspapers were printing full editions by week's end and addressed the indignation of some citizens: "The Journal has little sympathy with those who seem inclined to object to the rule of the military authorities. In a crisis like this, government must necessarily be strict … we should all bear with them with patience and courtesy." [92]   Ironically, there is no "police state" when the police are in charge of maintaining public order but when the military fulfills that role, the rules of engagement are different.

Throughout this second week of the recovery, the river levels continued to drop. Only a week earlier the river was at its highest stage at 28 feet but it had since plunged to 5.4 feet. It rose again to 10.2 feet by Saturday, April 5, but it would settle at a more normal level of 5.2 feet by the following Tuesday. [93]

Soldiers marching on Ludlow Street between Fifth and Sixth Streets

At the end of the week, there were 2,431 troops in Dayton. They guarded unprotected homes that were vacated during the worst of the storm and were keeping looters from stealing "trainloads of supplies pouring into the city from every direction." [94] On the interior, the soldiers were greatly assisted by the volunteer guards and citizen police who were sworn into temporary service by General Wood. These men were vital to the security of the city. There were no lights illuminating fully exposed buildings at night. The flood had shattered windows and dislodged doors leaving the contents of businesses vulnerable to thieves in the darkness.

Trainload of relief supplies delivered to Dayton

While the military patrolled the flood district outside, these civilian police guarded the buildings inside. Amos Crow, who had wholly lost his restaurant on South St. Clair Street, was on duty late at night on April 5 at a department store on East Fifth Street. Taking a moment to write his thoughts, he observed, "It is now ten o'clock Saturday night. I am all alone on police duty. I have charge of a large department store from six o'clock at night until six tomorrow morning. I have five floors to look after. I make the round all over the store every hour. There is no store closed up as all the windows are broken and a great amount of goods washed away and the mud is awful. The floor is covered about 6 inches with that sticky and oily mud you can not imagine the condition ...." [95]

The success of the arrangement between police, citizen guards and the military was best demonstrated by the orderly, active restoration of business places and homes. By Monday, April 7, two weeks into the recovery, 14 companies comprised of 600 men were able to be relieved from duty. This cut down the number of infantrymen patrolling the central city streets to 1,500. "This marked the second big withdrawal of troops for the city. The first occurred ... when conditions at Cincinnati were such that several companies were rushed from Dayton to that city." [96]

At the start of the third week a conference was held between military command and the heads of the police force. On Tuesday, April 8, the decision was made to start the orderly transfer of "territory" from the control of the soldiers in the field to police patrolmen including "... all territory lying south of Mad River, and east and south of the general line of Detroit Street to LaBelle, Richard, Wayne, Oak, Brown and Apple to the Miami River ... [as well as] the territory covering Riverdale north of the flooded districts and Dayton View ..., [in addition to] the territory west of the submerged district in Miami City and Edgemont." [97] Some Dayton police officers were also reassigned into the downtown district to handle traffic control and enforcement.

Assessing conditions: John Patterson (pointing) and Gen.George Wood (standing right)

As a result, 200 additional troops were relieved from duty and returned to their home stations of Toledo and Springfield. Safety Director Alberts Dodds reported: "Considering the havoc caused by the recent flood, the police and fire department were in good condition. Only one man, City Fireman Doudna lost his life." [98]   City Council was inclined at this stage in the recovery to evaluate financial appropriations for the safety services, and the city at large, but Mayor Philipps recommended "that the matter be delayed."

The timing of the transition of security duties from soldiers back to police was prompted in part to the reopening of the police Patrol House on Sears Street. It was back in operation on Wednesday, April 9. Much of the debris was removed although there were some repairs yet to be done. The press reported: "The place was filled with junk following the flood, but the building has been cleaned and telephone communication established." [99]

Notwithstanding the progress, on that very day local businessmen and professionals expressed grave reservations that the drawing down of troops was happening too rapidly. Martial law suited their interest by ensuring their properties were well guarded.

They appealed to Governor Cox to keep the community protected by halting the reduction of National Guardsmen. They firmly believed "the police department, because of insufficient numbers, [was] unable to cope with the local situation." [100]

"Open for Business" despite debris outside the Reibold Building on South Main Street

In spite of the fact that an estimated 1700 troops were still on duty in the city, they feared further withdrawals of the soldiers would leave the community at risk to looters. The Dayton Police Department was "handicapped by unsettled conditions [and] cannot give protection needed ...," they insisted and further opined, "Under favorable conditions the motorcycle squad could handle the work ... but because of the number of telephones not yet in working order, the bad condition of many of the streets, the squad would be handicapped." [101] Businessmen understood that the Gamewell system had become embedded in day-to-day patrol operations. Absent the system's full operation, emergency police communications was essentially nonexistent.

The National Guard had well protected the city at the time of its greatest peril and vulnerability. In one instance, when two men were caught by the military pillaging unsecured buildings, they were taken before Chief Allaback. Perturbed by the disruption, the Chief made his position quite clear to the soldiers when he said, "Don't bring looters to me. Kill them if you catch them looting." [102] The feared looting in the city was minimal; virtually unfounded. The military's mission was coming to a close.

Police had maintained order in the outskirts of downtown. It never relinquished its arrest authority and continued to assert its duties when there was probable cause to do so. The press was quick to report successful law enforcement activities. On Wednesday of week three, four men "believed to be thugs from Chicago" carrying concealed knives were arrested at Union Station by Dayton police following a fight. Officer George Klinger reported the "thugs" were "making themselves obnoxious and grabbing everything in sight." They were booked at the county jail. [103]

Relief supplies unloaded along the railroad track

78

The following day, Dayton police detectives began an investigation of a beating death at the Big Four railroad at Findlay Street. The victim suffered a broken neck and concussion. His body was removed to the temporary morgue at 217 West Third Street. "Brawls" had broken out between members of a gang of "hoboes" living in a railroad box car over large quantities of stolen whiskey. Around noon, Sgt. William Johnson and a police squad rounded up the gang in the railroad yard, conveying them to the county jail. [104]

General George H. Wood

General Wood was still administering to interior security and those arrested were adjudicated through military tribunal. Citizens were reassured that both the National Guardsmen and patrolmen were safeguarding the city in coordinated efforts. Front-line protection was augmented by investigatory work, best demonstrated by "Detectives Moore and Shibley" (believed to be Dayton officer Thomas L. Moore and county deputy John H. Shiveley). While conducting house-to-house canvassing *"working under military directions,"* the detectives uncovered stolen property, including a large amount of rings and pins, three barrels of coal oil, plumber tools, and a dozen boats. The confiscated items were stored at the Algonquin hotel. [105]

The city's recovery was proceeding at a remarkable rate given the devastation. By the end of week three, city and utility services were fast returning to normal. The main natural gas lines in the city were again operating, allowing citizens to heat their homes and cook meals. The speed by which the city was reclaimed from the catastrophe could be attributed to the comprehensive efforts of its many citizens.

General Wood noted that "during the first four days of the flood and before the arrival of any considerable portion of the Ohio National Guard, many citizens of Dayton volunteered their services [to protect their community] …." As a sign that the security of Dayton had reached a benchmark, on Saturday, April

12, the military commander issued General Order No. 37 to signal that it was heading back to the police: "All obligations incumbent upon volunteer guards, special deputies, and citizen police sworn in as such, since March 25, 1913, are hereby released and all appointments as such are void." [106]

It had been a brutal three weeks for all and the members of the safety services had taken a beating as well. In advocating for these men, one local newspaper took up the call of the public: "There is hardly a policeman or fireman in the whole city of Dayton who has a good or complete uniform .... Many of the men, now garbed in tattered uniforms, wear those clothes because they have no others .... [and even though policemen and firemen] are public servants and naturally are expected to engage in hard and heroic work ... the fact that they have been on constant duty for three weeks appears to have been lost sight of .... Many have suggested that the city should equip each officer and fireman who lost his uniform during the flood and fire with an entire new outfit." [107] Another local paper was to the point: "The heroism of the members of the police and fire departments in their remarkable work of rescue ..., while their own families were suffering, will never be forgotten." [108]

Lone National Guardsman on watch outside the Stomps-Burkhardt Company Chair Warehouse on E. Second and Canal Streets - *Dayton History*

The number of soldiers detailed to the city was reduced to 500 with the passing of another week but with orders on

Wednesday, April 23 that "most of the Dayton companies will be held on duty for several weeks, after martial law has been lifted, to act as special police." [109]

On Sunday, curfew was eased by four hours to 11:00 p.m. Saloons were allowed to stay open a half hour later until 6:30 p.m., prompting a delegation of ministers to protest the extended drinking time (the temperance movement was impassioned in 1913 and would lead to the legal prohibition of alcohol only seven years later).

"Curfew 6:30 P.M." sign outside the Elder &Johnston Co. on South Main Street
From the Dayton History Collection

On Monday morning, April 28, the military headquarters was transferred from the Algonquin hotel to the Y.M.C.A. across West Third Street (today City Hall). All criminal investigation trials remained under the jurisdiction of the military court. "The last of the out of town troops left the city ... and only the three local companies [patrolled the diminishing] martial district, bounded by the river, canal and railroad." [110]

With the withdrawal, Dayton Safety Director Mays Dodds made an appeal to the city's finance committee "in order that the efficiency of this police department ... be increased so that it can cope with the situation after the soldiers now on duty have been relieved." He wanted 30 additional patrolmen added on a temporary basis of about two months. [111] No police record suggests this personnel request was granted.

The month of April came to a close but by the first Sunday of May, the citizens' relief committee, headed by Chief Allaback, agreed it was time for Governor James Cox to lift his emergency declaration. The committee communicated with the Ohio governor its conditional request to "relieve the troops at present on duty in Dayton Tuesday morning, but that martial law be allowed to prevail for a matter of two weeks ...." [112]

The committee further attempted to convince the state leader to continue with the curfew period "from 11 o'clock at night until 4:30 o'clock in the morning [under martial law]; that General Wood remain ... in command [over the city's security]; and that the police take charge of the city in place of the soldiers." [113]

The group wanted the police to be able to "act as soldiers with the military regulations." That request was *not* approved by the governor: "All of the duties performed by the militia in the city since martial law was declared, will be resumed by the civil authorities." [114] Curfews hours and other necessary conditions, he insisted, could be established through the enactment of city ordinances.

Military camp on East Fifth Street at Findlay Street

Marking the seven-week anniversary of the worst natural disaster in Dayton's history, Governor Cox issued a proclamation.

Martial law would end in the city on Tuesday, May 6, when "all troops on duty … will be relieved and sent home by order of Adjutant General George H. Wood, acting by direction of the Governor."

Soldiers on South Main Street lookng north preparing to depart

The authority of the military had been in place for 42 days. This ended "the longest tour of duty performed by Ohio troops in state service since the civil war." [115]

Police sergeant and officer (foreground on right) during relief campaign outside the Court House - *From the Dayton History Collection*

83

Epilogue

1913 - 1922

Dayton **police badge,** top-break pocket pistol and police ledger
Photograph by Off. Amy M. Simpson

Epilogue: 1913 - 1922

On Tuesday, May 6 at 8:00 in the morning, the "Dayton military district" ceased to exist by General Order No. 51. Adjutant General George Wood praised his soldiers: "The work during the first few weeks of this tour of duty was arduous and difficult. The city was in complete darkness, doors were open, windows were without glass and property of all kinds was unprotected. In spite of all of these facts, no authenticated case of looting has been brought to these headquarters." [116]

That sense of appreciation was sincerely felt by the soldiers' civilian counterpart. "The work of the military was [also] praised by Chief Allaback, a former regular army man, who went through the Indian Wars." [117] The 2,400 troops maintained public order and safeguarded citizens in cooperation with many civilian volunteer deputies and the 136 sworn members of the Dayton police force.

John H. Patterson (second left) and Gen. George H. Wood
(second right) traveling with others

In the *instant* aftermath of the 1913 Great Flood, police patrol changed little but, over the course of time, the Great Flood would usher in profound changes to local law enforcement. It would also be a major transformative event for the municipal government and for those living in the city as well.

Beginning in 1913, N.C.R. founder *John Patterson* took it upon himself to save Dayton and rebuild it as a first rate city (one with fewer horses but a certain future tied to the automobile industry). The other leaders who had been with Patterson at the time of this local crisis moved on with their lives.

Patterson was behind the efforts to establish a new charter for the city of Dayton. As a major element to the change, Dayton became the nation's first major city to adopt the "commission-city manager" form of government, replacing a "strong mayor" approach. The charter became effective October 1913 at a time that *Mayor Edward Philipps'* term in office, coincidently, came to an end (although he continued to reside in the city and work as a debt collector). Patterson also led the efforts to create the Miami Conservancy District, ensuring a comprehensive flood protection plan was forever in place. It was completed in 1922 and was the first of its kind in the world. It remains an engineering archetype duplicated in large river valleys throughout the United States and worldwide.

Receded flood waters on Keowee Street at the Barney & Smith Company

The Great Flood caused many local businesses, *large and small*, to forever close. The Barney & Smith Company was one of the largest builders of *wooden* train cars in the nation. The plant complex was terribly damaged but it was as much a victim of its failure to modernize in 1905 – when it failed to enter the *steel* freight car market – as it was from the harsh thrashing of 1913. The flood, though, sealed its fate. The company went into receivership, came out in 1915 but "the gates were closed in February 1921." [118]

The same ruin was handed the smaller Makley & Stomps Livery, which went out of business due to the catastrophe. Its owner was also affected by modernization; however, he chose to embrace it. Although in 1913 "horses were still used a great deal ..., after the flood in which hundreds of horses were drowned, the automobile almost totally replaced them." [119] One of the co-owners, Gustave Stomps, saw this future. He started a new business selling Lexington automobiles and then changed in 1916 to a Chevrolet dealership. In 1928, he had a Stomps Chevrolet building erected alongside the site of the recently razed old City Workhouse. Dayton's first Chevrolet dealership would prosper for 50 years.

From the Dayton History Collection

Dayton City Workhouse (1876 – 1926)
South Main & West Sixth Streets
Stomps Chevrolet (1927 – 1968)

From the Dayton History Collection

89

John Patterson's National Cash Register Company came away from the Great Flood unscathed. Its factories too thrived for over 50 years. It was a cornerstone of industry in Dayton. N.C.R. fostered engineering innovators, Colonel Edward Deeds and Charles Kettering, who together formed Dayton Engineering Laboratories Company (Delco). General Motors later acquired Delco and firmly established GM industrial plants throughout the city. The automobile industry flourished in Dayton for 50 years and the population of the city more than doubled to a mid-1960s estimate of 267,000. Eventually, by the 1970s, N.C.R., General Motors, Delco and even the smaller Stomps business would experience the fading of their local successes but from conditions other than flood waters.

Many of the decision-makers from 1913 took on other pursuits. *A. Mays Dodds*, who had appealed for an increase of 30 police officers on a temporary basis, served out 1913 as his last year as Dayton's safety director. He would move on to the Cleveland area and find employment in the automobile industry. In 1916, *General George Wood* entered two-years active military duty in France during the Great War and then return to serve as president of the board of managers of Soldiers Home in Dayton until 1930.

James Cox and Franklin Roosevelt campaigning in Dayton

In November 1913, the Dayton Daily News, owned by *Governor James Cox*, began publishing its Sunday edition.

The rival Dayton Herald newspaper, which had advocated for new uniforms for police officers to replace the "tattered" ones, was the first of the three local papers to stop publishing. In 1948, Cox purchased both the Herald and rival Dayton Journal, merging the two (the *Journal Herald* went out of print when it combined with the Dayton Daily News 40 years later). In 1920, Governor Cox, in the company of his vice presidential running mate, Franklin D. Roosevelt, was greeted by the citizens of his hometown of Dayton while engaged in an unsuccessful campaign for the United States presidency.

In 1913, with the enactment of Dayton's new city charter, the police force officially became the *Division* of Police under the Department of Public Safety, which also oversaw the *Division* of Fire and *Division* of Telegraph & Signals. The latter of the three would not only manage the Gamewell and fire alarm systems, but would be instrumental with the development of traffic signal systems for motor vehicles. *Fire Chief Frank Ramby* continued in his post until 1935, one of Dayton's longest-serving fire chiefs.

Continuing in his post, *Police Chief John Allaback* guided the Division of Police through the rest of the decade into the 1920s. The manpower of the Dayton police force gradually returned to 160 sworn personnel and then increased to 177 by 1920. The authorized sworn strength would continue to rise relative to Dayton's fast increasing population, but it seemed to always lag behind in adequate staffing (criticism for this by the local newspapers remained a recurring theme with each passing decade).

One proposal that had been made by Mays Dodds coming out of the 1913 Flood was that "the 12-hour shift ... be abolished and the eight-hour shift substituted. The majority of the policemen have been on duty 12 hours a day since the flood ... and deserve shorter hours." [120] That in fact happened in keeping with a national trend initiated in 1914 by the Ford Motor Company and then furthered by the 1915 federal Adamson Act. In due course, the Dayton patrolmen's work week was also reduced from seven to six days.

Dayton police officers wearing crisp uniforms, Pershing-style hats and leather puttees

By 1914, the style of police uniforms changed. Whether the city absorbed the costs as recommended by the newspaper is undetermined. Nevertheless, patrolmen no longer wore bobby-style hats, instead adopting the "Pershing" hat, much like the style that is worn today. The officers also began wearing black leather puttees covering their shins and calves. It would be another 18 years before they would wear black leather gun belts with covered gun holsters visible to the public.

Although not all changes to the police force were a direct result of the Great Flood, the timing of this Dayton tragedy coincided with the many reforms that were occurring in society at large. And cultural changes always influence the nature of policing.

Locally, the Flood Relief Commission brought in more than $2 million (in 1913 dollars). One woman, Elizabeth Richter, donated $1,500 to the flood relief fund, according to a "record book in the conservancy office," [121] an amount equal to $35,000 in 2013 dollars. That woman also answered to the name Lib Hedges. She was the infamous local madam, owner of many homes of ill repute. Despite the generous financial contributions she made to the flood relief effort, and after years of society closing its eyes to it, the public demanded that houses of prostitution be aggressively targeted by police and closed down. They were, with vigor.

Policewoman Lulu Sollers (tall lady center) and Police Model T Ford

Local law enforcement in 1913 was not unlike policing throughout the nation; it was strictly a *male-only* occupation. In June 1914, Dayton's first Policewomen's Bureau was established when the first city manager brought to town a settlement worker from Chicago and placed her in charge. Often confused as being the jail matrons, policewomen were assigned to the Department of Public Safety and dressed in civilian attire but wore a badge.

Annie McCulley
First Policewoman

Their basic duties were to check dance halls for wayward girls and to warn young girls of the "soldier boys" that were in town. Over time, policewomen would investigate juvenile crimes and assist vice detectives in proactive enforcement measures. It was not until 60 years later, in 1974, that women were assigned uniform patrol duties on the streets of Dayton.

The police force created a bicycle unit in 1914 as the golden age of bicycles came to an end. The intent was to further expand its mobile patrol capabilities and augment the motorcycle squad, which proved its worth during the Great Flood. The less expensive two-wheelers only lasted until 1916 because responses to emergency calls were often slowed by policemen having to repair punctured tires. This method of patrol was resurrected in 1990 with great success and continues to this day.

Dayton bicycle squad (1914 – 1916) wearing new Pershing-style hat

The police force ended its 30-year use of horse-drawn wagons and 20-year use of horses for patrol by 1914, although a nine-member mounted patrol unit was resurrected in 1989. It remained popular until it was abolished in 2003 due to budgetary constraints. On August 26, 1915 the Dayton police force acquired its first automobile, a Model T Ford. The horse-drawn wagons and ambulance were replaced with motorized vehicles. By 1920, the police force had four Model Ts – the "Ford Squad" – two motorized wagons, a Cadillac, and a high-powered vehicle used by its traffic "speed officer."

Motorized paddy wagon and police ambulance (Ptl. Frank Johnson seated inside) at **Patrol House**   *Courtesy of Carolyn J. Burns, granddaughter of Ptl. Johnson*

Societal progress in the first few years after the Great Flood was not without some grave drawbacks. One of the most tragic years in Dayton police history was 1916. A police officer was killed every four months. In January, Ptl. John Stapleton was killed when his police motorcycle slammed into the side of a motorized fire engine. Despite the growing success of the temperance movement, Ptl. Charles Thomas was shot to death in May while chasing a bootlegger; and Ptl. George Purcell was shot three times and killed in September while questioning a suspect at a saloon about a concealed firearm.

Patrolman Stapleton

Patrolman Thomas

Patrolman Purcell

By 1920, the 90-year temperance movement was triumphant and soon erased the city of Dayton's 230 saloons [122] from the landscape. Prohibition was instituted with ratification of the 18th Amendment to the United States Constitution, intensifying bootlegging and making it – and associated crimes – even more dangerous to law enforcement officers.

Dayton Patrolman busting a still

Prohibition and the Great Depression brought new challenges and controversies for the police and the memories of the dauntless actions taken by Dayton patrolmen during the Great Flood receded, like the waters, in a relative brief time.

Dayton Police Model T Ford Squad

Chief John Allaback – who was appointed to the police force in 1886, promoted to chief in 1908, and directed his force through the ordeals brought on by the 1913 Great Flood – witnessed the acquisition of a new Central Police Station, replacing the one "condemned" before the flood and made worse by it. Finally, in 1921 police officers moved into the building constructed on South Ford Street, just east of the old Patrol House on Sears Street (both are now vacant lots near the Dayton Dragons Fifth-Third Field).

Dayton police officers in their *new* uniforms with a *new* arsenal
and *new* automobile at their *new* **Central Police Station**
on South Ford Street between Webster and Sears Streets
Courtesy of Carolyn J. Burns (Ptl. Frank Johnson center)

Chief John Allaback had earned this gratifying achievement for his men in blue. As Dayton's longest-serving leader with 15 years in command, the chief never sought to retire. But he left the police force on October 29, 1922, nearly 10 years after the Great Flood.

While still serving and protecting the citizens of Dayton as their chief of police, John Allaback died in office at age 64.

Postscript:
Gamewell System of Police Telegraph

A **patrol call box** amid flood wreckage,
affixed to its iron stanchion.

Postscript: Gamewell System of Police Telegraph
and the advance of police communications systems

In 1883, soon after telephone service was established in the city, the Dayton Police Department had telephone boxes installed for patrolmen at a dozen locations throughout the city. Box "No. 9" was located in Riverdale at North Main and Babbitt Streets.

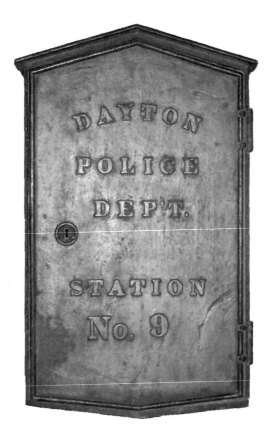

In 1896, the Gamewell System of Police Telegraph was instituted and enhanced in 1902. Patrol call boxes were the primary means of direct communication between patrolman and police "central exchange" operator (see page 36).

This method of communication was used by officers on walking beat assignments for nearly 70 years until the introduction of portable radios.

During the time of the **1913 Great Flood**, patrolmen could use a call box key inserted in the "Wagon Call" key hole to send a telegraph signal identifying their location or actually open the box to call in to the central police exchange.

Police communication technology advanced from whistles (1870s), to patrol call boxes (1890s), to one-way patrol car radio reception (1932), to two-way police cruiser radio transmission (1940), to hand-held portable radios (1964) to in-car keyboard display terminals (1986), to today's mobile data terminals (MDT).

Photographs by Officer Amy Simpson

Endnotes

1   "Dayton And Her Government: Police 1797–1877," *Facet* (monthly City of Dayton publication), February 1966.

2   Joseph W. Sharts, *The Biography of Dayton*, "Part Three, Chapter III, Politics - The Evolution of Police Protection" (Dayton, Ohio: The Miami Valley Socialist, 1922), p. 84.

3   Meeting minutes (regular session): Dayton City Council, Monday, February 27, 1911 (C. N. Greer, Secretary, Reference---Finance). Research courtesy of David Klippel (great grandson of Capt. Edward Poland).

4   Journal: Patrolman Edward F. Poland (assigned the Third Precinct), journal entries: 15 June 1911 and 1 July 1911.

5   Op. cit., Sharts, p. 85.

6   Dayton Police Department records (multiple Dayton police source documents): "Dayton Police Dayton, Ohio Illustrated" (1910), "Department of Safety, Dayton, Ohio Division of Police" photo collage (1917), and other corroborating general Dayton Police records (1910-17) including departmental unsourced documents.

7   Ibid., Dayton Police records.

8   "Two Patrolmen Return to Duty," *The Dayton Daily News*, 17 April 1913.

9   Curt Dalton, *Through Flood, Through Fire: Personal Stories from Survivors of the Dayton Flood of 1913* (C. Dalton: Dayton, Ohio: Mazier Corporation, 2001), Chapter: "Floods in Dayton Prior to 1913" (M. E. Curwen).

10 Allan W. Eckert, *A Time of Terror: The Great Dayton Flood* (Toronto: Little, Brown & Company, Ltd, 1965), p. 9.

11 Ibid., p. 14.

12 Ibid., p. 15.

13 J. David Rogers, *The 1913 Dayton Flood and the Birth of Modern Flood Control Engineering in the United States* (Natural Hazards Mitigation Institute: University of Missouri-Rolla), Internet, 16 Dec. 2012, <http://web.mst. edu/~rogersda/umrcourses/ge301/dayton%20flood-updated.pdf>.

14 Op. cit., Eckert, p. 15.

15 Ibid., p. 21.

16 Ibid., p. 16.

17 Ibid., p. 35.

18 Ibid., p. 53.

19 Film: *Goodbye, The Levee Has Broken, The Story of the Great Dayton Flood,* produced by Think[TV] in partnership with the Montgomery County Historical Society, 2005.

20 Op. cit., Eckert, p. 53.

21 Ibid., p. 63.

22 "Have Narrow Escapes in Warning Others," *The Dayton Journal*, 2 April 1913.

23 Op. cit., Eckert, p. 63.

24 "Sears Street Patrol House About Ready," *The Dayton Journal*, 7 April 1913.

25 Edgar Allen Forbes, "The Man on the Job at Dayton", *Leslie's Illustrated Weekly Newspaper,* May 8, 1913.

26 "Strenuous Times for City Firemen and Police Force," *The Dayton Evening Herald*, 15 April 1913.

27 "Police and Firemen Are Heavy Losers," *The Dayton Daily News*, 14 April 1913.

28 George H. Wood, *Report of General George H. Wood on the Dayton Flood* (Springfield, Ohio: "Annual Report of the Adjutant General to the Governor of the State of Ohio for the year ending November 15, 1913", 1914), "Part One - March 25th to March 31st, 1913."

29 "Police Returning to Former Beats," *The Dayton Evening Herald*, 14 April 1913.

30 Op. cit., Wood, "Part One – March 25th to March 31st, 1913".

31 Op. cit., "Have Narrow Escapes in Warning Others."

32 "Last Alarm," Posted 27 Aug. 2011, Dayton IAFF Local 136, Internet 23 Dec. 2012, <http://www.iaff136.org/?zone=unionactive/view_page.cfm&page=Last20Alarm>.

33 "Patrolman Carries People to Safety," *The Dayton Journal*, 2 April 1913.

34 Op. cit., *Goodbye, The Levee Has Broken*.

35 John Calvin Hover, ed., Joseph D. Barnes, ed., et al., *Memoirs of The Miami Valley*, "Volume II" (Chicago: Robert O. Law 6ompany, 1920), pp. 73-74.

36 Op. cit., Wood, "Part One – March 25th to March 31st, 1913".

37 "Brave Acts of Officers Are Praised," *The Dayton Journal*, 3 April 1913.

38 "Little Sidelights on Disaster Which Had Been Overlooked in Rush for News," *The Dayton Journal*, 3 April 1913.

39 "Judge Owes Life to Policemen's Work," *The Dayton Journal*, 3 April 1913.

40 Op. cit., Eckert, p. 61.

41 George H. Wood, *Report of General George H. Wood on the Dayton Flood* (Springfield, Ohio: "Annual Report of the Adjutant General to the Governor of the State of Ohio for the year ending November 15, 1913", 1914), "Part Two – April 1st to May 6th, 1913".

42 Op. cit., Eckert, p. 169.

43 Alice Lingo Conger, "FLOOD of 1913—A Dairy," *The Dayton Daily News*, 23 March 23, 1986.

44 "Run for the hills! Wall of water rushing down river!", *Flood March 1913*, Internet 26 Dec. 2012, <http://www.lanepl.org/scanned/FLOOD/flood%20 8-14.pdf>, p. 8.

45 Ibid., pp. 10-12.

46 Postcard: "Reassuring Message, Dayton, Ohio", Floods of 1913, Published by Haenlein Bros., Cincinnati, Ohio, Internet 26 Dec. 2012, <http://brisray. com/flood/fpcards11.htm>.

47 Letter from Amos Crow to "Mother & Father" written on The Fair stationary (The S. & M. Margolis Co., 28-30 East Fifth Street, Dayton, Ohio), 5 April 1913. Letter provided courtesy of Judge Daniel Gehres (relative of Amos Crow).

48 Harry Rogers, Manuscript: *Before the Flood*, 1962, Internet, 16 Dec. 2012, <http://www.daytonhistorybooks.com/page/page/5001519.htm>.

49 Ibid.

50 Op. cit., *Goodbye, The Levee Has Broken*.

51 A.H. Horton and H.J. Jackson, "The Ohio Valley Flood of March-April 1913", United States Geological Survey of the Department of the Interior, Water- Supply Paper 334 (Government Printing Office, Washington D.C., 1913), p. 26.

52 Op. cit., *Goodbye, The Levee Has Broken*.

53 "Patrolman Injured By A Falling Board," *The Dayton Journal*, 11 April 1913.

54 "Police and Firemen Crippled By Mishaps," *The Dayton Journal*, 13 April 1913.

55 "Police Officer Succumbs to the Virulent Malady," *The Dayton Journal,* 20 Feb. 1914.

56 "Patrolman Conway Dies," *The Dayton Daily News*, 20 Feb. 1914.

57 Op. cit., Wood, "Part One – March 25th to March 31st, 1913".

58 Ibid.

59 Op. cit., "Strenuous Times for City Firemen and Police Force."

60 "Dayton Beginning to Get Reliable Knowledge of Conditions, Finds Some Hope in Situation," *Waterloo Times Tribune*, Waterloo, Iowa, 28 March 1913.

61 Op. cit., *Goodbye, The Levee Has Broken.*

62 "Only 200 Persons Lost Lives in Dayton According to Estimate of the Police Chief," *The Constitution,* Atlanta, Georgia, 28 March 1913.

63 "Mayor Phillips and Family Safe," [*sic*] *The Dayton Daily News*, 29 March 1913.

64 Op. cit., "Dayton Beginning to Get Reliable Knowledge ...."

65 "Fatality List Cut Down When Exploration is Made," *Waterloo Evening Courier,* Waterloo, Iowa, 29, March 1913.

66 Op. cit., Letter from Amos Crow.

67 Trudy E. Bell, *The Great Dayton Flood of 1913* (Chicago; Arcadia Publishing), copyright © 2008, p. 10.

68 "Dayton Facing Situation with Wonderful Bravery," *The Dayton Daily News*, (Flood Extra, Issued from the Offices of the National Cash Register Company), 28 March 1913.

69 Montgomery County Death Certificate No. 19578, Catharine Grundish, 29 March 1913.

70 Tom Grundish (grandson of Dayton Police Inspector Thomas Grundish), "Inspector Grundish", e-mails to Stephen Grismer, 21 Feb. 2013 & 21 Feb. 2013.

71 "George Clinger Killed," *The Dayton Daily News*, 29 March 1913. [Note: Officer Klinger's last name was misspelled in the newspaper article and the officer's first name was used in error in headline and story in identifying his deceased brother.]

72 "Ohio's Flood Toll is Placed at 454 Lives," *The Dayton Journal*, 6 April 1913.

73 Op. cit., *Goodbye, The Levee Has Broken.*

74 Telegram from Uncle Ray (Dayton) to Dickie, The Postal Telegraph-Cable Company (Incorporated), 20 April 1913.

75 Op. cit., Letter from Amos Crow.

76 Beth Grismer SND (cover by Lloyd Ostendorf), *The Stomps-Griesemer Family History*, "Part One - The Stomps Family Line" (reference William Makley & Gustave Stomps Livery), copyright © 1984, p. 26.

77 Op. cit., "Dayton Facing Situation with Wonderful Bravery."

78 Compilation of the Ordinances, of the Common Council of the Town of Dayton, Published by Authority, An Ordinance to Prevent Nuisances, Sec. 3 (R.J. Skinner, Printer, Dayton) 1826.

79 Jack Barstow (grandson of Dayton Police Chief Rudolph Wurstner), "More Background on Chief Wurstner", e-mail to Stephen Grismer, 19 May 2008.

80 "Bicycle Club Completes Fine Work; 1250 Dead Horses Removed," *The Dayton Journal*, 3 April 1913.

81 Op. cit., Wood, "Part Two – April 1st to May 6th, 1913".

82 Op. cit., A.H. Horton and H.J. Jackson.

83 Op. cit., "Police Returning to Former Beats."

84 "Police Department Now on Regular Duty," *The Dayton Journal*, 2 April 1913.

85 Board of Police Directors, *25th Annual Report of the Department of Police of the City of Dayton for the Fiscal Year Ending February 28, 1898* (J. W. Johnson, Dayton, Ohio 1898), p. 6.

86 Ibid., *25th Annual Police Report (1897-98)*, T. J. Farrell, "Report of the Superintendent", p. 11.

87 "Hurrah! Central Police Station May Be Closed," *The Dayton Journal*, 3 April 1913.

88 "70,000 Still Marooned at Dayton–Revolt in Workhouse," *The Washington Post*, Washington D.C., Friday, 28 March 1913.

89 "Where Fire and Flood Played Havoc, as Seen Through the Camera of Journal Photographer," *The Dayton Journal*, 2 April 1913.

90 "Indiana Situation is Well in Hand," *Daily Commonwealth*, Fond Du Lac, Wisconsin, 28 March 1913.

91 "Motorcycle Squad Does Relief Work," *The Dayton Daily News*, 9 April 1913.

92 "Military Rule," *The Dayton Journal*, 5 April 1913.

93 Op. cit., A.H. Horton and H.J. Jackson.

94 "Nearly 2,500 Guardsmen Are Still on Duty in Dayton," *The Dayton Journal*, 6 April 1913.

95 Op. cit., Letter from Amos Crow.

96 "Troops Leaving Dayton As City Gains Strength," *The Dayton Journal*, 8 April 1913.

97 Op. cit., Wood, "Part Two – April 1st to May 6th, 1913".

98 "Mayor Asks Delay in Appropriations," *The Dayton Journal*, 9 April 1913.

99 "Sears Street Patrol House Again In Use," *The Dayton Journal*, 10 April 1913.

100 "Asks an Addition of 30 Policemen to City's Force," *The Dayton Evening Herald*, 3 May 1913.

101 "Governor Petitioned to Keep Troops Here," *The Dayton Journal*, 10 April 1913.

102 Marshall Everett, *The Tragic Story of America's Greatest Disaster*. (Chicago, J.S. Ziegler Company, 1913). "Orders Looters Killed." P. 177

103 "Rough House Party Quelled by Police," *The Dayton Journal*, 10 April 1913.

104 "Officers Nab Gang of Hoboes and Seize Quantity of Whiskey," *The Dayton Evening Herald*, 10 April 1913.

105 "Detectives Recover Many Costly Rings," *The Dayton Evening Herald*, 21 April 1913.

106 Op. cit., Wood, "Part Two – April 1st to May 6th, 1913".

107 Op. cit., "Strenuous Times for City Firemen and Police Force."

108 Op. cit., "Police and Firemen Are Heavy Losers."

109 "Militia is Reduced 200 Men; 500 Remain," *The Dayton Journal*, 23 April 1913.

110 "Curfew Extended Following Order of Governor Cox – Barrooms Now to Keep Open Until 6:30 p.m., Ministers Protest," *The Dayton Evening Herald*, 28 April 1913.

111 Op. cit., "Asks an Addition of 30 Policemen to City's Force."

112 "Police to Assume the Same Power as the Soldiers," *The Dayton Evening Herald*, 3 May 1913.

113 Ibid.

114 "Reign of Martial Law in Dayton Will End Tuesday," *The Dayton Evening Herald*, 5 May 1913.

115 Ibid.

116 "Military Law Finally Off; City Back Again to Normal," *The Dayton Evening Herald*, 6 May 1913.

117 "Praises Military," *The Dayton Journal*, 2 April 1913.

118 "Builders of Wooden Railway Cars ... and some of other stuff," Posted 9 April 2006, *Barney & Smith Manufacturing Company*, Internet 5 Jan. 2013, <http://www.midcontinent.org/rollingstock/builders/barney-smith.htm>, p. 2.

119 Op. cit., Rogers.

120 Op. cit., "Asks an Addition of 30 Policemen to City's Force."

121 Roz Young, "Bessie and Lizzie", *The Dayton Journal Herald*, 21 Oct. 1972.

122 *Williams' Dayton Directory for 1913-14* (The Williams Directory Company; publishers, Cincinnati © 1913), "Saloons," pp. 1548-1549.

Photographs

The photographs appearing in this book are courtesy of the Dayton Metro Library, Carolyn J. Burns, Dayton History and the Dayton Police History Foundation, Inc. collection. One particular photograph that stands out is an early image of Dayton motorcycle officers on page 73, donated to DPH Foundation in 2012 by Jimmy Greger, the grandson of Ptl. Otha E. Greger (1906-1938). Ptl. Greger is standing fourth from right in the motorcycle photo. He rose to the rank of police inspector in his career.

Patrolman Greger

Retired Montgomery County Sheriff's Deputy Mike Friedman and retired Dayton Firefighter Bill Sayer facilitated the acquisition of photographs for Dayton Police History Foundation, Inc.

In 2011 on behalf of DPH Foundation, Dayton Police Officer Amy Simpson gave countless hours to photograph police artifacts from many different eras in Dayton police history as well as fellow police officers clothed in period uniforms. Several of those photographs appear as the introduction to chapters of this book and on the front cover. Those photos are captioned herein and include the names of the subjects of her lens.

Carolyn J. Burns made available a number of early police photographs in which her grandfather appears. One of her photos introduces Part 4. Two others are featured in the Epilogue. A number of photographs of flood scenes and the city of Dayton are from the Dayton History collection and reprinted with the expressed permission of Mary Oliver, director of collections. The Dayton History and Carolyn Burns photographs are credited beneath the images and captions.

All other photographs shown without attribution are either from the collections of the Dayton Metro Library or Dayton Police History Foundation, Inc.

Dayton Police History Foundation, Inc.

Dayton Police History Foundation, Inc. is an outgrowth of a 2008 six-month police exhibit at Carillon Historical Park, *Patrolling the Streets of Dayton*. It was the largest temporary exhibit held at the park's newest museum facility at that time, the Dicke Family Transportation Center. It was visited by 20,000 school students and, by that measure alone, was a success.

Dayton Police History Foundation, Inc. was officially chartered by the State of Ohio on January 1, 2010. It is a non-profit, 501(c)(3) charitable organization strictly dedicated to the preservation of local police history.

DPH Foundation, Inc. is an independent organization operating in cooperation with the city of Dayton Police Department, the Dayton Fraternal Order of Police, the Dayton History-NCR Archive Center, Carillon Historical Park and many other organizations. More can be learned about DPH Foundation at the following website:

www.DaytonPoliceHistory.org

Contact or Comment:
info@DaytonPoliceHistory.org

Donations to support the efforts of DPH Foundation, Inc. are gratefully accepted and receipted. Please mail to:

DPH Foundation, Inc.
P.O. 293157
Dayton, Ohio 45429-9157

About the Author

 Sgt. Stephen Grismer (ret.) is a 25-year veteran of the Dayton Police Department. He entered the police academy in 1976 and was later assigned to uniform patrol duties in the Fifth District. Promoted in 1986, he experienced a broad career in investigations, staff, internal affairs, drug enforcement, intelligence and training. He was a member of the hostage negotiation team, the vice president of the Dayton Fraternal Order of Police and an FOP official in a variety of roles from 1988 to present day. He is a 1984 graduate of the University of Dayton with a degree concentration in journalism and a minor in criminal justice. In 2008 he helped produce the successful police exhibit at Carillon Historical Park, *Patrolling the Streets of Dayton*. Currently, he is a member of the Dayton Police History Foundation, Inc. Board of Trustees.

Made in the USA
Columbia, SC
01 April 2022

58385567R00064